SCHOLASTIC
W9-CHJ-694

Let's Find Out

Let's Have Fun
With Alphabet Riddles

Caolan Madden

Scholastic Inc.
New York Toronto London Auckland Sydney
Mexico City New Delhi Hong Kong Buenos Aires

Literacy Specialist: Francie Alexander, Chief Academic Officer, Scholastic Inc.
Art Director: Joan Michael

Photographs: James Levin

ISBN 0-439-91577-5

2 3 4 5 6 7 8 9 10   62   19 18 17 16 15 14

There are alphabet riddles
All through this book.
Do you think you can solve them?
Come take a look!

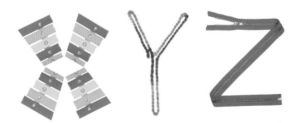

It's red and it's sweet.
It grows on a tree.
It starts with an A.
Crunch, munch—what can it be?

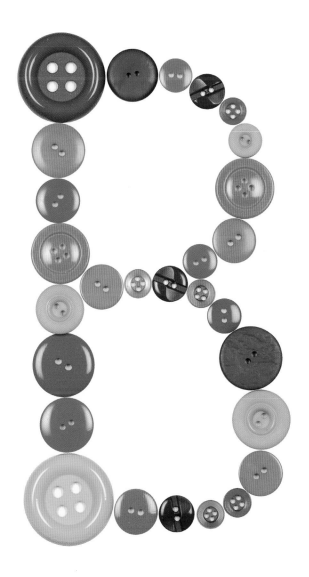

It is sewn to a sweater,
A coat, or a dress.
It starts with a B.
What's it called? Can you guess?

It can drive on a road.
Vroom! It races on by.
It starts with a C.
Can you name it? Just try!

It can make a big mess.
Flowers need it to grow.
It starts with a D.
What's it called? Do you know?

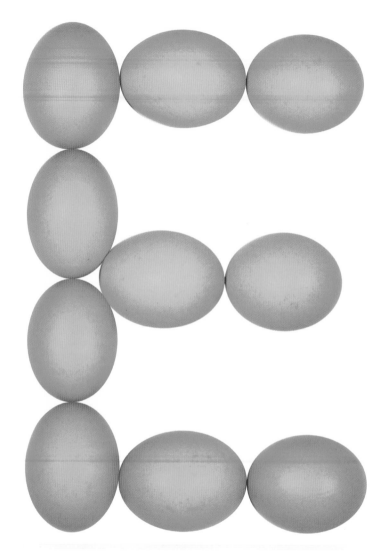

It has a hard shell.
It is easy to fry.
It starts with an E.
Can you name it? Just try.

They cover a bird's wings.
They're soft and so light.
They start with an F.
Name them now. Were you right?

They are squishy and sweet.
A vine's where they grow.
They begin with a G.
What are they? Do you know?

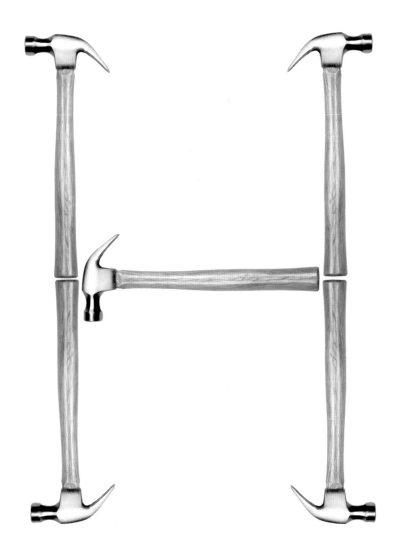

It's a tool you can build with.
Its handle is wood.
It starts with an H.
Can you guess? That is good!

It crawls or it flies.
Six legs help it go.
It begins with an I.
What's it called? Do you know?

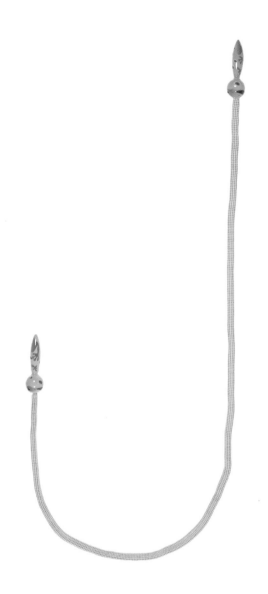

It's long and it's skinny.
Children use it to play.
It starts with a J.
What's it called? Can you say?

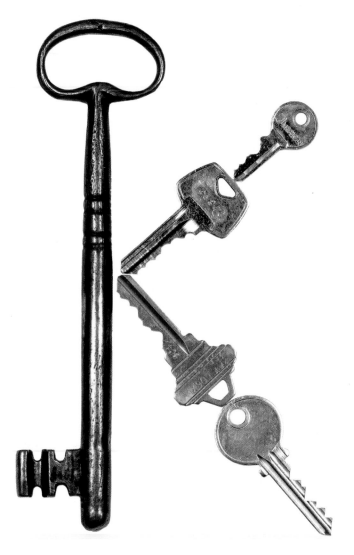

It can lock up a door,
Then unlock it, you see.
It starts with a K.
Oh, what can it be?

In the spring, it is green.
In the fall, it turns red.
It starts with an L.
What's it called? Use your head!

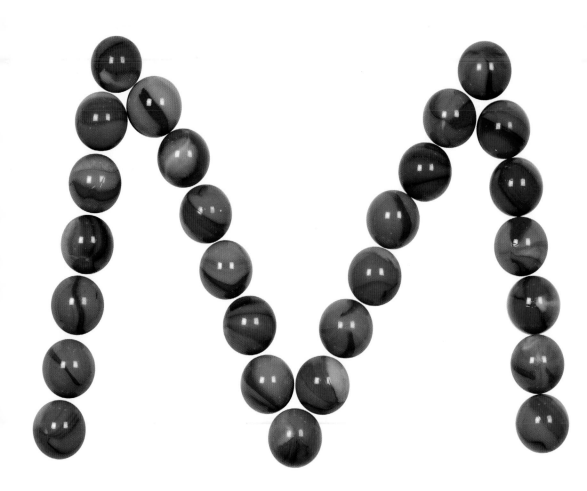

It's smooth and it's round.
You can roll it about.
It starts with an M.
What's it called? Let's find out!

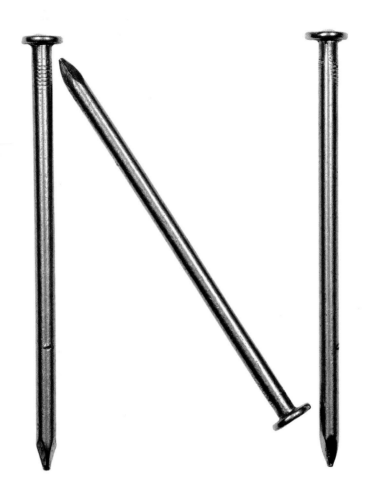

It is flat on the top
And pointy below.
It begins with an N.
What's it called? Do you know?

They are salty and green.
They come in a jar.
They begin with an O.
Can you guess what they are?

It's light and it's fluffy.
It's good for a snack.
It starts with a P.
Guess—you're on the right track!

It's cozy and comfy.
It covers a bed.
It starts with a Q.
What's it called? Use your head!

It's heavy and hard.
It's black, brown, or gray.
It starts with an R.
What's its name? Can you say?

It will keep your neck warm
When the wind starts to blow.
It starts with an S.
What's it called? Do you know?

It travels on tracks.
It goes "Choo-Choo" all day.
It begins with a T.
What's it called? Can you say?

When you walk in the rain,
It will keep your head dry.
It begins with a U.
Can you name it? Just try!

It's a small purple flower
That grows in the spring.
It begins with a V.
Can you name this thing?

Here is something that's cut
From the trunk of a tree.
It begins with a W.
Oh, what can it be?

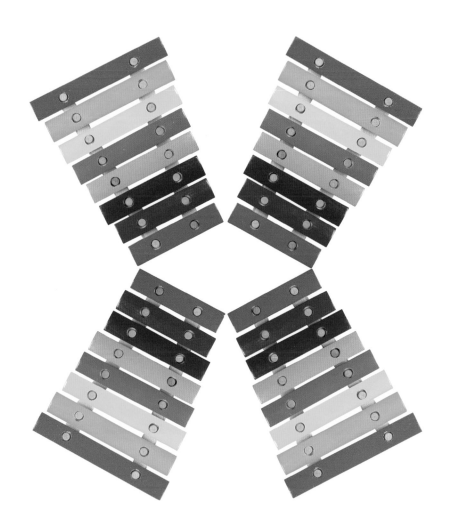

It makes pretty music.
It's so fun to play.
It begins with an X.
What's it called? Can you say?

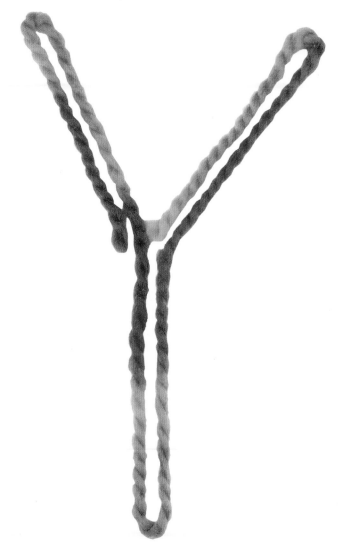

It is thicker than thread.
People use it to knit.
It begins with a Y.
Try to guess—what is it?

It can close up your backpack
As quick as a wink.
It begins with a Z.
What's it called, do you think?

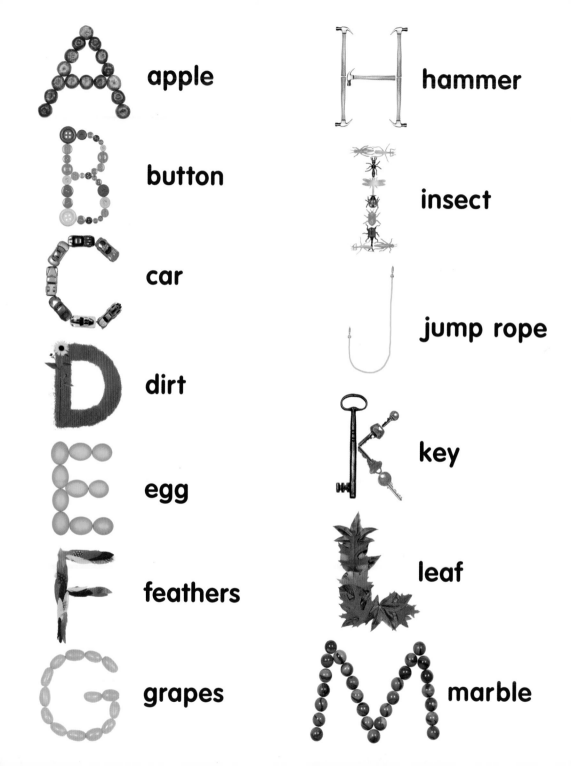

apple

button

car

dirt

egg

feathers

grapes

hammer

insect

jump rope

key

leaf

marble

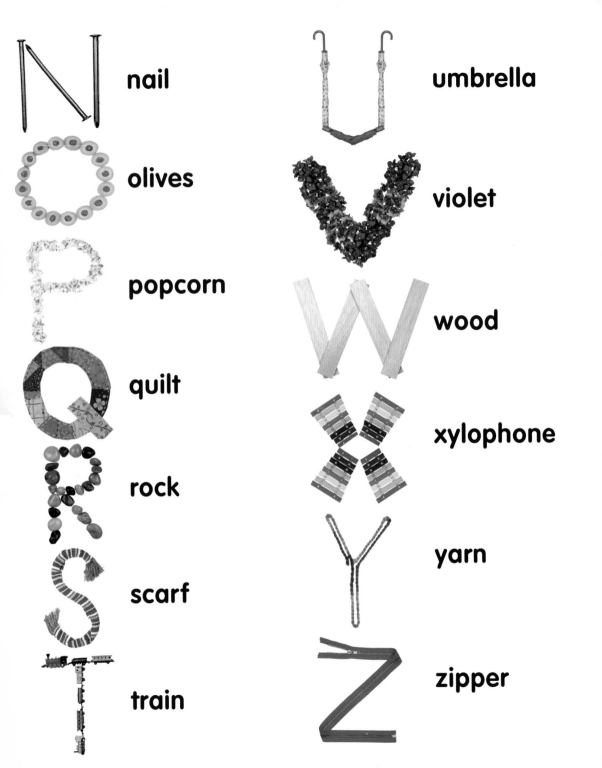

nail

olives

popcorn

quilt

rock

scarf

train

umbrella

violet

wood

xylophone

yarn

zipper

Can you name all the things that you saw in this book?
Do you know their first letters?
Go back and look!

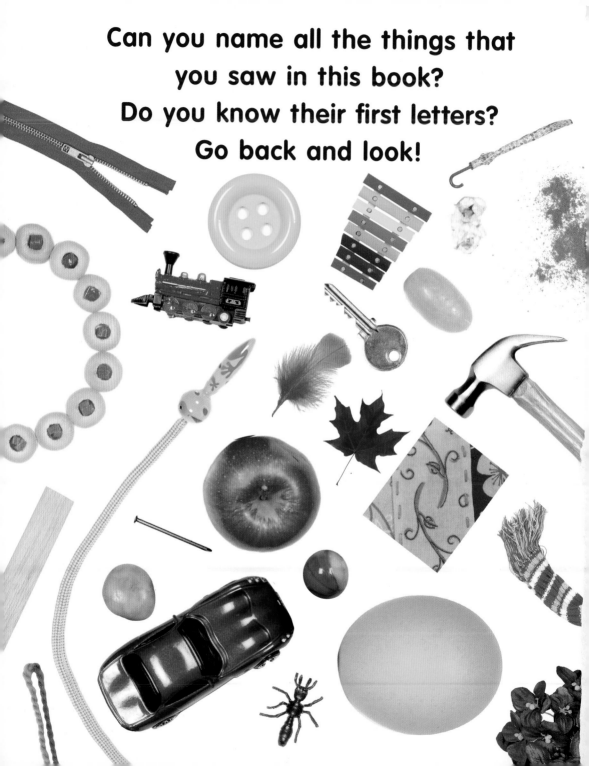